The Ultimate Time Maximization Tool

Weekly Planner for Men

Activinotes

DAILY JOURNALS, PLANNERS, NOTEBOOKS AND OTHER BLANK BOOKS

Do not pray for an easy life, Pray for the to endure a difficult one.

Believe in yourself a little

Weekly Planner for Men

monday

time	Schedule

tuesday

time	Schedule

wednesday

time	Schedule

thursday

time	Schedule

friday

time	Schedule	time	Schedule

Weekly Planner for Men

saturday

time	Schedule

sunday

time	Schedule

things to do:

_____

_____

_____

_____

_____

_____

work-out schedule:

-
-
-
-
-

things to buy:

_____

_____

_____

_____

_____

_____

_____

important appointments:

-
-
-
-
-

Weekly Planner for Men

monday

time	Schedule

tuesday

time	Schedule

wednesday

time	Schedule

thursday

time	Schedule

friday

time	Schedule	time	Schedule

Weekly Planner for Men

saturday

time	Schedule

sunday

time	Schedule

things to do:

_____

_____

_____

_____

_____

_____

_____

work-out schedule:

-
-
-
-
-

important
   appointments:

-
-
-
-
-

things to buy:

_____

_____

_____

_____

_____

_____

_____

Weekly Planner for Men

monday

time	Schedule

tuesday

time	Schedule

wednesday

time	Schedule

thursday

time	Schedule

friday

time	Schedule	time	Schedule

Weekly Planner for Men

saturday	
time	Schedule

sunday	
time	Schedule

things to do:

_____

_____

_____

_____

_____

_____

_____

work-out schedule:

-
-
-
-
-

things to buy:

_____

_____

_____

_____

_____

_____

important appointments:

-
-
-
-
-

Weekly Planner for Men

monday

time	Schedule

tuesday

time	Schedule

wednesday

time	Schedule

thursday

time	Schedule

friday

time	Schedule	time	Schedule

Weekly Planner for Men

saturday

time	Schedule

sunday

time	Schedule

things to do:

_____

_____

_____

_____

_____

_____

_____

work-out schedule:

-
-
-
-
-

things to buy:

_____

_____

_____

_____

_____

_____

important
   appointments:

-
-
-
-
-

Weekly Planner for Men

monday

time	Schedule

tuesday

time	Schedule

wednesday

time	Schedule

thursday

time	Schedule

friday

time	Schedule	time	Schedule

Weekly Planner for Men

saturday

time	Schedule

sunday

time	Schedule

things to do:

_____
_____
_____
_____
_____
_____
_____

work-out schedule:

-
-
-
-
-

things to buy:

_____
_____
_____
_____
_____
_____

important appointments:

-
-
-
-
-

Weekly Planner for Men

monday

time	Schedule

tuesday

time	Schedule

wednesday

time	Schedule

thursday

time	Schedule

friday

time	Schedule	time	Schedule

Weekly Planner for Men

saturday

time	Schedule

sunday

time	Schedule

things to do:
_____
_____
_____
_____
_____
_____
_____
_____

work-out schedule:
-
-
-
-
-

important
   appointments:
-
-
-
-
-

things to buy:
_____
_____
_____
_____
_____
_____
_____

Weekly Planner for Men

monday

time	Schedule

tuesday

time	Schedule

wednesday

time	Schedule

thursday

time	Schedule

friday

time	Schedule	time	Schedule

Weekly Planner for Men

saturday

time	Schedule

sunday

time	Schedule

things to do:

_____

_____

_____

_____

_____

_____

_____

work-out schedule:

-
-
-
-
-

things to buy:

_____

_____

_____

_____

_____

important appointments:

-
-
-
-
-

Weekly Planner for Men

monday

time	Schedule

tuesday

time	Schedule

wednesday

time	Schedule

thursday

time	Schedule

friday

time	Schedule	time	Schedule

Weekly Planner for Men

saturday	
time	Schedule

sunday	
time	Schedule

things to do:
_____
_____
_____
_____
_____
_____
_____

important
appointments:
-
-
-
-
-

work-out schedule:
-
-
-
-
-

things to buy:
_____
_____
_____
_____
_____
_____

Weekly Planner for Men

monday

time	Schedule

tuesday

time	Schedule

wednesday

time	Schedule

thursday

time	Schedule

friday

time	Schedule	time	Schedule

Weekly Planner for Men

saturday	
time	Schedule

sunday	
time	Schedule

things to do:

_____

_____

_____

_____

_____

_____

_____

work-out schedule:

-
-
-
-
-

things to buy:

_____

_____

_____

_____

_____

_____

important appointments:

-
-
-
-
-

Weekly Planner for Men

monday

time	Schedule

tuesday

time	Schedule

wednesday

time	Schedule

thursday

time	Schedule

friday

time	Schedule	time	Schedule

Weekly Planner for Men

saturday	
time	Schedule

sunday	
time	Schedule

things to do:

_____

_____

_____

_____

_____

_____

_____

work-out schedule:

-
-
-
-
-

things to buy:

_____

_____

_____

_____

_____

_____

important
appointments:

-
-
-
-
-

Weekly Planner for Men

monday

time	Schedule

tuesday

time	Schedule

wednesday

time	Schedule

thursday

time	Schedule

friday

time	Schedule	time	Schedule

Weekly Planner for Men

saturday

time	Schedule

sunday

time	Schedule

things to do:

_____

_____

_____

_____

_____

_____

_____

work-out schedule:

-
-
-
-
-

things to buy:

_____

_____

_____

_____

_____

_____

_____

important appointments:

-
-
-
-
-

Weekly Planner for Men

monday

time	Schedule

tuesday

time	Schedule

wednesday

time	Schedule

thursday

time	Schedule

friday

time	Schedule	time	Schedule

Weekly Planner for Men

saturday	
time	Schedule

sunday	
time	Schedule

things to do:

_____

_____

_____

_____

_____

_____

_____

work-out schedule:

-
-
-
-
-

important appointments:

-
-
-
-
-

things to buy:

_____

_____

_____

_____

_____

_____

Weekly Planner for Men

monday

time	Schedule

tuesday

time	Schedule

wednesday

time	Schedule

thursday

time	Schedule

friday

time	Schedule	time	Schedule

Weekly Planner for Men

saturday	
time	Schedule

sunday	
time	Schedule

things to do:

_____
_____
_____
_____
_____
_____
_____

work-out schedule:

-
-
-
-
-

things to buy:

_____
_____
_____
_____
_____
_____

important appointments:

-
-
-
-
-

Weekly Planner for Men

monday

time	Schedule

tuesday

time	Schedule

wednesday

time	Schedule

thursday

time	Schedule

friday

time	Schedule	time	Schedule

Weekly Planner for Men

saturday

time	Schedule

sunday

time	Schedule

things to do:

_____

_____

_____

_____

_____

_____

_____

work-out schedule:

-
-
-
-
-

things to buy:

_____

_____

_____

_____

_____

_____

important appointments:

-
-
-
-
-

Weekly Planner for Men

monday

time	Schedule

tuesday

time	Schedule

wednesday

time	Schedule

thursday

time	Schedule

friday

time	Schedule	time	Schedule

Weekly Planner for Men

saturday

time	Schedule

sunday

time	Schedule

things to do:

_____

_____

_____

_____

_____

_____

_____

work-out schedule:

-
-
-
-
-

things to buy:

_____

_____

_____

_____

_____

_____

important appointments:

-
-
-
-
-

Weekly Planner for Men

monday

time	Schedule

tuesday

time	Schedule

wednesday

time	Schedule

thursday

time	Schedule

friday

time	Schedule	time	Schedule

Weekly Planner for Men

saturday	
time	Schedule

sunday	
time	Schedule

things to do:

_____

_____

_____

_____

_____

_____

_____

work-out schedule:

-
-
-
-
-

things to buy:

_____

_____

_____

_____

_____

important appointments:

-
-
-
-
-

Weekly Planner for Men

monday

time	Schedule

tuesday

time	Schedule

wednesday

time	Schedule

thursday

time	Schedule

friday

time	Schedule	time	Schedule

Weekly Planner for Men

saturday	
time	Schedule

sunday	
time	Schedule

things to do:

_____

_____

_____

_____

_____

_____

_____

work-out schedule:

-
-
-
-
-

important appointments:

-
-
-
-
-

things to buy:

_____

_____

_____

_____

_____

_____

Weekly Planner for Men

monday

time	Schedule

tuesday

time	Schedule

wednesday

time	Schedule

thursday

time	Schedule

friday

time	Schedule	time	Schedule

Weekly Planner for Men

time	Schedule
saturday	

time	Schedule
sunday	

things to do:

_____

_____

_____

_____

_____

_____

_____

work-out schedule:

-
-
-
-
-

things to buy:

_____

_____

_____

_____

_____

_____

important appointments:

-
-
-
-
-

Weekly Planner for Men

monday

time	Schedule

tuesday

time	Schedule

wednesday

time	Schedule

thursday

time	Schedule

friday

time	Schedule	time	Schedule

Weekly Planner for Men

saturday	
time	Schedule

sunday	
time	Schedule

things to do:
_____
_____
_____
_____
_____
_____
_____
_____

work-out schedule:

-
-
-
-
-

important
   appointments:

-
-
-
-
-

things to buy:
_____
_____
_____
_____
_____
_____
_____

Weekly Planner for Men

monday

time	Schedule

tuesday

time	Schedule

wednesday

time	Schedule

thursday

time	Schedule

friday

time	Schedule	time	Schedule

Weekly Planner for Men

saturday	
time	Schedule

sunday	
time	Schedule

things to do:
_____
_____
_____
_____
_____
_____
_____

work-out schedule:
-
-
-
-
-

things to buy:
_____
_____
_____
_____
_____
_____

important
    appointments:
-
-
-
-
-

Weekly Planner for Men

monday

time	Schedule

tuesday

time	Schedule

wednesday

time	Schedule

thursday

time	Schedule

friday

time	Schedule	time	Schedule

Weekly Planner for Men

saturday	
time	Schedule

sunday	
time	Schedule

things to do:

_____

_____

_____

_____

_____

_____

_____

work-out schedule:

-
-
-
-
-

things to buy:

_____

_____

_____

_____

_____

_____

_____

important appointments:

-
-
-
-
-

Weekly Planner for Men

monday

time	Schedule

tuesday

time	Schedule

wednesday

time	Schedule

thursday

time	Schedule

friday

time	Schedule	time	Schedule

Weekly Planner for Men

saturday	
time	Schedule

sunday	
time	Schedule

things to do:
_____
_____
_____
_____
_____
_____
_____

work-out schedule:
•
•
•
•
•

important
    appointments:
•
•
•
•
•

things to buy:
_____
_____
_____
_____
_____
_____
_____

Weekly Planner for Men

monday

time	Schedule

tuesday

time	Schedule

wednesday

time	Schedule

thursday

time	Schedule

friday

time	Schedule	time	Schedule

Weekly Planner for Men

saturday	
time	Schedule

sunday	
time	Schedule

things to do:

_____

_____

_____

_____

_____

_____

_____

_____

work-out schedule:

-
-
-
-
-

things to buy:

_____

_____

_____

_____

_____

_____

_____

important
      appointments:

-
-
-
-
-

Weekly Planner for Men

monday

time	Schedule

tuesday

time	Schedule

wednesday

time	Schedule

thursday

time	Schedule

friday

time	Schedule	time	Schedule

Weekly Planner for Men

saturday	
time	Schedule

sunday	
time	Schedule

things to do:
_____

_____

_____

_____

_____

_____

work-out schedule:
•

•

•

•

•

important appointments:
•

•

•

•

•

things to buy:
_____

_____

_____

_____

_____

_____

Weekly Planner for Men

monday

time	Schedule

tuesday

time	Schedule

wednesday

time	Schedule

thursday

time	Schedule

friday

time	Schedule	time	Schedule

Weekly Planner for Men

saturday	
time	Schedule

sunday	
time	Schedule

things to do:
_____
_____
_____
_____
_____
_____
_____

work-out schedule:
-
-
-
-
-

important
    appointments:
-
-
-
-
-

things to buy:
_____
_____
_____
_____
_____
_____

Weekly Planner for Men

monday

time	Schedule

tuesday

time	Schedule

wednesday

time	Schedule

thursday

time	Schedule

friday

time	Schedule	time	Schedule

Weekly Planner for Men

saturday	
time	Schedule

sunday	
time	Schedule

things to do:

_____
_____
_____
_____
_____
_____
_____
_____

work-out schedule:

-
-
-
-
-

important appointments:

-
-
-
-
-

things to buy:

_____
_____
_____
_____
_____
_____
_____
_____

Weekly Planner for Men

monday

time	Schedule

tuesday

time	Schedule

wednesday

time	Schedule

thursday

time	Schedule

friday

time	Schedule	time	Schedule

Weekly Planner for Men

saturday

time	Schedule

sunday

time	Schedule

things to do:

_____
_____
_____
_____
_____
_____
_____

work-out schedule:

-
-
-
-
-

things to buy:

_____
_____
_____
_____
_____
_____

important appointments:

-
-
-
-
-

Weekly Planner for Men

monday

time	Schedule

tuesday

time	Schedule

wednesday

time	Schedule

thursday

time	Schedule

friday

time	Schedule	time	Schedule

Weekly Planner for Men

saturday	
time	Schedule

sunday	
time	Schedule

things to do:

_____

_____

_____

_____

_____

_____

_____

work-out schedule:

-
-
-
-
-

things to buy:

_____

_____

_____

_____

_____

_____

important appointments:

-
-
-
-
-

Weekly Planner for Men

monday

time	Schedule

tuesday

time	Schedule

wednesday

time	Schedule

thursday

time	Schedule

friday

time	Schedule	time	Schedule

Weekly Planner for Men

saturday

time	Schedule

sunday

time	Schedule

things to do:

_____

_____

_____

_____

_____

_____

_____

work-out schedule:

-
-
-
-
-

things to buy:

_____

_____

_____

_____

_____

_____

important appointments:

-
-
-
-
-

Weekly Planner for Men

monday

time	Schedule

tuesday

time	Schedule

wednesday

time	Schedule

thursday

time	Schedule

friday

time	Schedule	time	Schedule

Weekly Planner for Men

saturday	
time	Schedule

sunday	
time	Schedule

things to do:

_____

_____

_____

_____

_____

_____

_____

work-out schedule:

-
-
-
-
-

important appointments:

-
-
-
-
-

things to buy:

_____

_____

_____

_____

_____

_____

_____

Weekly Planner for Men

monday

time	Schedule

tuesday

time	Schedule

wednesday

time	Schedule

thursday

time	Schedule

friday

time	Schedule	time	Schedule

Weekly Planner for Men

saturday	
time	Schedule

sunday	
time	Schedule

things to do:
_____
_____
_____
_____
_____
_____
_____

work-out schedule:

-
-
-
-
-

important
    appointments:

-
-
-
-
-

things to buy:
_____
_____
_____
_____
_____
_____
_____
_____

Weekly Planner for Men

monday

time	Schedule

tuesday

time	Schedule

wednesday

time	Schedule

thursday

time	Schedule

friday

time	Schedule	time	Schedule

Weekly Planner for Men

saturday

time	Schedule

sunday

time	Schedule

things to do:
_____
_____
_____
_____
_____
_____
_____

work-out schedule:
-
-
-
-
-

important
   appointments:
-
-
-
-
-

things to buy:
_____
_____
_____
_____
_____
_____
_____

Weekly Planner for Men

monday

time	Schedule

tuesday

time	Schedule

wednesday

time	Schedule

thursday

time	Schedule

friday

time	Schedule	time	Schedule

Weekly Planner for Men

saturday	
time	Schedule

sunday	
time	Schedule

things to do:

_____
_____
_____
_____
_____
_____
_____
_____

work-out schedule:

-
-
-
-
-

important appointments:

-
-
-
-
-

things to buy:

_____
_____
_____
_____
_____
_____
_____

Weekly Planner for Men

monday

time	Schedule

tuesday

time	Schedule

wednesday

time	Schedule

thursday

time	Schedule

friday

time	Schedule	time	Schedule

Weekly Planner for Men

saturday	
time	Schedule

sunday	
time	Schedule

things to do:
_____
_____
_____
_____
_____
_____
_____

work-out schedule:

-
-
-
-
-

things to buy:
_____
_____
_____
_____
_____

important appointments:

-
-
-
-
-

Weekly Planner for Men

monday

time	Schedule

tuesday

time	Schedule

wednesday

time	Schedule

thursday

time	Schedule

friday

time	Schedule	time	Schedule

Weekly Planner for Men

saturday	
time	Schedule

sunday	
time	Schedule

things to do:
_____
_____
_____
_____
_____
_____
_____

work-out schedule:
-
-
-
-
-

important appointments:
-
-
-
-
-

things to buy:
_____
_____
_____
_____
_____
_____
_____

Weekly Planner for Men

monday

time	Schedule

tuesday

time	Schedule

wednesday

time	Schedule

thursday

time	Schedule

friday

time	Schedule	time	Schedule

Weekly Planner for Men

saturday	
time	Schedule

sunday	
time	Schedule

things to do:
_____
_____
_____
_____
_____
_____
_____
_____

work-out schedule:
-
-
-
-
-

things to buy:
_____
_____
_____
_____
_____
_____
_____

important
   appointments:
-
-
-
-
-

Weekly Planner for Men

monday

time	Schedule

tuesday

time	Schedule

wednesday

time	Schedule

thursday

time	Schedule

friday

time	Schedule	time	Schedule

Weekly Planner for Men

saturday	
time	Schedule

sunday	
time	Schedule

things to do:

_____

_____

_____

_____

_____

_____

_____

work-out schedule:

-
-
-
-
-

things to buy:

_____

_____

_____

_____

_____

_____

_____

important appointments:

-
-
-
-
-

Weekly Planner for Men

monday

time	Schedule

tuesday

time	Schedule

wednesday

time	Schedule

thursday

time	Schedule

friday

time	Schedule	time	Schedule

Weekly Planner for Men

saturday

time	Schedule

sunday

time	Schedule

things to do:

_____

_____

_____

_____

_____

_____

_____

work-out schedule:

-
-
-
-
-

things to buy:

_____

_____

_____

_____

_____

important
    appointments:

-
-
-
-
-

Weekly Planner for Men

monday

time	Schedule

tuesday

time	Schedule

wednesday

time	Schedule

thursday

time	Schedule

friday

time	Schedule	time	Schedule

Weekly Planner for Men

saturday	
time	Schedule

sunday	
time	Schedule

things to do:

_____
_____
_____
_____
_____
_____
_____

work-out schedule:

-
-
-
-
-

things to buy:

_____
_____
_____
_____
_____
_____

important
    appointments:

-
-
-
-
-

Weekly Planner for Men

monday

time	Schedule

tuesday

time	Schedule

wednesday

time	Schedule

thursday

time	Schedule

friday

time	Schedule	time	Schedule

Weekly Planner for Men

saturday	
time	Schedule

sunday	
time	Schedule

things to do:
_____
_____
_____
_____
_____
_____
_____

work-out schedule:
-
-
-
-
-

things to buy:
_____
_____
_____
_____
_____

important
    appointments:
-
-
-
-
-

Weekly Planner for Men

monday

time	Schedule

tuesday

time	Schedule

wednesday

time	Schedule

thursday

time	Schedule

friday

time	Schedule	time	Schedule

Weekly Planner for Men

saturday

time	Schedule

sunday

time	Schedule

things to do:

_____

_____

_____

_____

_____

_____

_____

work-out schedule:

-
-
-
-
-

things to buy:

_____

_____

_____

_____

_____

_____

_____

important
    appointments:

-
-
-
-
-

Weekly Planner for Men

monday

time	Schedule

tuesday

time	Schedule

wednesday

time	Schedule

thursday

time	Schedule

friday

time	Schedule	time	Schedule

Weekly Planner for Men

saturday	
time	Schedule

sunday	
time	Schedule

things to do:

_____

_____

_____

_____

_____

_____

_____

work-out schedule:

•

•

•

•

•

things to buy:

_____

_____

_____

_____

_____

_____

important
    appointments:

•

•

•

•

•

Weekly Planner for Men

monday

time	Schedule

tuesday

time	Schedule

wednesday

time	Schedule

thursday

time	Schedule

friday

time	Schedule	time	Schedule

Weekly Planner for Men

saturday	
time	Schedule

sunday	
time	Schedule

things to do:
_____
_____
_____
_____
_____
_____
_____

work-out schedule:
-
-
-
-
-

things to buy:
_____
_____
_____
_____
_____
_____

important appointments:
-
-
-
-
-

Weekly Planner for Men

monday

time	Schedule

tuesday

time	Schedule

wednesday

time	Schedule

thursday

time	Schedule

friday

time	Schedule	time	Schedule

Weekly Planner for Men

saturday

time	Schedule

sunday

time	Schedule

things to do:
_____
_____
_____
_____
_____
_____
_____

work-out schedule:
-
-
-
-
-

important
   appointments:
-
-
-
-
-

things to buy:
_____
_____
_____
_____
_____
_____

Weekly Planner for Men

monday

time	Schedule

tuesday

time	Schedule

wednesday

time	Schedule

thursday

time	Schedule

friday

time	Schedule	time	Schedule

Weekly Planner for Men

saturday	
time	Schedule

sunday	
time	Schedule

things to do:

_____

_____

_____

_____

_____

_____

_____

work-out schedule:

•

•

•

•

•

things to buy:

_____

_____

_____

_____

_____

_____

_____

important
   appointments:

•

•

•

•

•

Weekly Planner for Men

monday

time	Schedule

tuesday

time	Schedule

wednesday

time	Schedule

thursday

time	Schedule

friday

time	Schedule	time	Schedule

Weekly Planner for Men

saturday

time	Schedule

sunday

time	Schedule

things to do:

_____

_____

_____

_____

_____

_____

_____

work-out schedule:

-
-
-
-
-

things to buy:

_____

_____

_____

_____

_____

_____

important
    appointments:

-
-
-
-
-

Weekly Planner for Men

monday

time	Schedule

tuesday

time	Schedule

wednesday

time	Schedule

thursday

time	Schedule

friday

time	Schedule	time	Schedule

Weekly Planner for Men

saturday	
time	Schedule

sunday	
time	Schedule

things to do:
_____
_____
_____
_____
_____
_____
_____
_____

work-out schedule:

-
-
-
-
-

things to buy:
_____
_____
_____
_____
_____
_____
_____

important
    appointments:

-
-
-
-
-

Weekly Planner for Men

monday

time	Schedule

tuesday

time	Schedule

wednesday

time	Schedule

thursday

time	Schedule

friday

time	Schedule	time	Schedule

Weekly Planner for Men

saturday	
time	Schedule

sunday	
time	Schedule

things to do:

_____

_____

_____

_____

_____

_____

_____

work-out schedule:

-
-
-
-
-

things to buy:

_____

_____

_____

_____

_____

_____

_____

important appointments:

-
-
-
-
-

Weekly Planner for Men

monday

time	Schedule

tuesday

time	Schedule

wednesday

time	Schedule

thursday

time	Schedule

friday

time	Schedule	time	Schedule

Weekly Planner for Men

saturday	
time	Schedule

sunday	
time	Schedule

things to do:
_____
_____
_____
_____
_____
_____
_____

work-out schedule:
-
-
-
-
-

important appointments:
-
-
-
-
-

things to buy:
_____
_____
_____
_____
_____
_____
_____

Weekly Planner for Men

monday

time	Schedule

tuesday

time	Schedule

wednesday

time	Schedule

thursday

time	Schedule

friday

time	Schedule	time	Schedule

Weekly Planner for Men

saturday	
time	Schedule

sunday	
time	Schedule

things to do:

_____

_____

_____

_____

_____

_____

_____

work-out schedule:

-
-
-
-
-

important appointments:

-
-
-
-
-

things to buy:

_____

_____

_____

_____

_____

_____

Weekly Planner for Men

monday

time	Schedule

tuesday

time	Schedule

wednesday

time	Schedule

thursday

time	Schedule

friday

time	Schedule	time	Schedule

Weekly Planner for Men

saturday	
time	Schedule

sunday	
time	Schedule

things to do:
_____
_____
_____
_____
_____
_____
_____

work-out schedule:
-
-
-
-
-

things to buy:
_____
_____
_____
_____
_____
_____
_____

important
      appointments:
-
-
-
-
-

Weekly Planner for Men

monday

time	Schedule

tuesday

time	Schedule

wednesday

time	Schedule

thursday

time	Schedule

friday

time	Schedule	time	Schedule

Weekly Planner for Men

saturday

time	Schedule

sunday

time	Schedule

things to do:
_____
_____
_____
_____
_____
_____
_____

work-out schedule:
-
-
-
-
-

things to buy:
_____
_____
_____
_____
_____
_____

important
   appointments:
-
-
-
-
-

www.ingramcontent.com/pod-product-compliance
Lightning Source LLC
Chambersburg PA
CBHW081333090426
42737CB00017B/3117